Tea

'I could do with a nice cup of tea!' This everyday phrase sums up the benefits we expect from this popular drink. Tea is reviving, relaxing and refreshing. Tea is also big business. Some 1.8 million tonnes of it are produced each year around the world. About 40 per cent of this is exported, earning much needed money for producer-countries. Britain is the largest importer, with its caterers earning over £3 million each day from the sale of cups of tea. This book takes a detailed look at the tea industry, examining all the stages involved from tea leaf to tea cup, as well as discussing the fascinating history of this beneficial beverage. Alan Blackwood was an editor of children's books before becoming a freelance author. He has written numerous books for a variety of publishers.

Tea

'I could do with a nice cup of tea!' This everyday phrase sums up the benefits we expect from this popular drink. Tea is reviving, relaxing and refreshing. Tea is also big business. Some 1.8 million tonnes of it are produced each year around the world. About 40 per cent of this is exported, earning much needed money for producer-countries. Britain is the largest importer, with its caterers earning over £3 million each day from the sale of cups of tea. This book takes a detailed look at the tea industry, examining all the stages involved from tea leaf to tea cup, as well as discussing the fascinating history of this beneficial beverage. Alan Blackwood was an editor of children's books before becoming a freelance author. He has written numerous books for a variety of publishers.

Focus on
TEA

Alan Blackwood

Focus on Resources series

Alternative Energy
Coffee
Cotton
Dairy Produce
Gas
Grain
Nuclear Fuel
Oil
Seafood
Sugar
Tea
Timber
Water
Wool

Frontispiece *Tea pickers at work on a hillside plantation in Sri Lanka.*

First published in 1985 by
Wayland (Publishers) Ltd
49 Lansdowne Place, Hove
East Sussex BN3 1HF, England

© Copyright 1985 Wayland (Publishers) Ltd

ISBN 0 85078 549 9

Phototypeset by Kalligraphics Ltd, Redhill, Surrey
Printed in Italy by G. Canale & C.S.p.A., Turin
Bound in the UK by The Bath Press

Contents

1. What is tea?

'Tea' can mean almost any drink made by soaking, or infusing, certain substances in hot water. So, we can have nettle, mint or camomile tea, types of herbal tea that are supposed to be very good from a health point of view.

For most of us, though, tea means the blackish-brown powdery substance we buy in packets, or in little perforated paper bags, which we brew up with boiling water. Its main ingredients are tannin, which gives the drink its amber colour, and caffeine. This latter substance, also found in coffee, makes tea a stimulant, which is why people like a cup of tea to freshen or wake them up.

This tea – one of the most popular drinks in

Pickers working along the neat rows of tea on a plantation in Sri Lanka.

This handful of freshly picked tea leaves has to go through several processes before it can produce the flavoursome beverage that we all enjoy.

the world – comes from the leaves of a plant called originally by the Latin name of *thea sinensis*, but now better known as *camellia sinensis*. In its wild state, it grows into a handsome tree about 5 to 9 metres (15 to 30 feet) tall, with bright green leaves, and small, mildly fragrant white flowers. But, as we shall read, the plants from which we get our packet tea have

been cultivated as rows of small bushes.

If we picked leaves straight off a tree or bush of *camellia sinensis* and brewed them up, we still would not get a beverage that tasted much like the drink we know and enjoy. The secret of tea, as we shall also read shortly, lies in the special way the leaves are treated, after they have been gathered.

2. Where tea is grown

There are several varieties of *camellia sinensis*, each of which grows best in different conditions. For example, the type of bush traditionally grown in China is suited to cooler temperatures during the winter months than varieties of the plant that produce what are called Indian or Assam trees.

Having said this, varieties of *camellia sinensis* all share much the same basic requirements for healthy growth. First of all, they need a comparatively warm climate for most or all of the year — frost would quickly damage or destroy them altogether. This limits their cultivation to certain tropical or sub-tropical regions of the world.

On the other hand, tea plants do not like

Inside an Iranian tea factory.

Tea being picked on Java, in Indonesia.

extremes of heat or too much fierce sunlight. Above all, they do need plenty of rain – somewhere between 2,300 mm and 5,000 mm (about 90 to 200 inches) per year – and a fairly moist atmosphere.

For all these reasons, most varieties of tea grow best in the hilly areas of the tropics – up to an altitude of around 2,000 metres (between 6,000 and 7,000 feet). The hills are cooler than the plains, and generally receive more rain.

Also, up in the cooler, moister hill country of many tropical regions, there is less risk of storms than down on the baking hot plains. Violent winds, torrential rain or hail could easily damage tender young tea bushes.

Main tea-producing countries in the world
(Estimated annual production in thousand metric tonnes; 1 metric tonne = 1,000 kilograms; 1 kilogram =2.2lb)

1	India	550
2	China	277
3	Sri Lanka	206
4	Turkey	165
5	USSR	115
6	Kenya	99
7	Japan	98
8	Indonesia	73
9	Bangladesh	36
10	Malawi	33
11	Argentina	32
12	Taiwan	27
13	Iran	21
14	Mozambique	20
15	Tanzania	18
16	Uganda	11

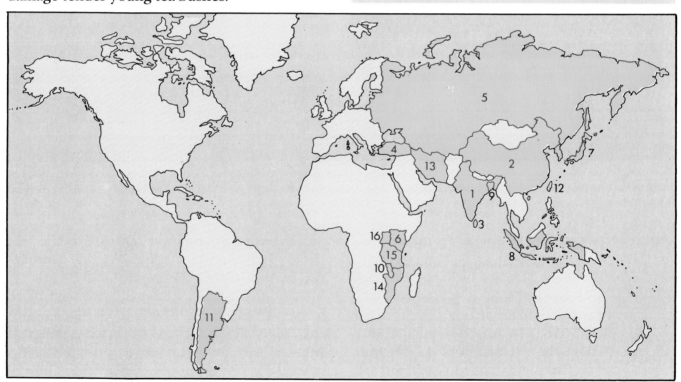

3. Soil erosion

A picker at work on the steep slopes of a tea plantation in the Cameron Highlands of Peninsular Malaysia.

Mention of wind and rain raises the problems of soil erosion – the carrying away of soil and earth by wind or water. This is a problem for many farmers, and especially for tea planters, who cultivate the steep slopes of hills.

It is most serious when a new plantation is being started. The young plants do not have strong roots. This means they do not 'bind' the soil together. So, when it rains there is a real danger that the water will carry away the top-soil as it runs down the slope.

Planting the bushes along the contours of the slope – that is, along the line of the slope rather than up or down the side of the hill – helps to prevent this. So does planting another crop among the young bushes. Oats is often chosen,

Terraces of tea bushes on a hillside in Sri Lanka. The terraces prevent the rain washing the soil away.

because it grows quickly and does not take too much goodness out of the soil, while helping to bind it together.

Planting trees among the bushes is another good idea. The roots bind the soil, while the trees themselves provide useful shade for the bushes, and protect them against too much wind.

One of the oldest farming practices in hilly country is to build the land up into terraces, or steps of land. This is also one of the best of all safeguards against erosion. The rain falls on the level surface of each terrace and soaks into the soil, instead of running straight down the hillside, taking precious earth with it. Many tea plantations are terraced.

11

4. Pests and diseases

The chemical make-up of the soil is equally important for growing tea. Some soils are naturally alkaline. Others have more acid in them. This latter type suits tea plants best.

One way of keeping the soil acid is by feeding it with a compost made from the leaves of the tea plants themselves. This needs to be done regularly, as compost is soon chemically broken up in the warm, moist soil of most tea plantations.

The young plants also need plenty of nitrogen – the basic 'food' of all plant life. The right kind of fertilizers put back into the soil the nitrogen used up by the plants. Phosphorus and potassium added to the soil in the right amounts also help to produce strong, healthy tea plants

Below left *The shot-hole borer beetle bores into the stem of tea plants (lower drawing) to lay its eggs.* **Below right** *The scarlet mite is a serious pest on Sri Lankan tea plantations.*

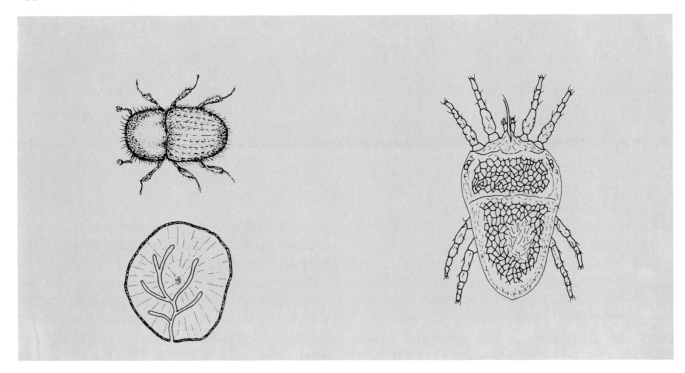

Workers on a plantation in China spraying tea bushes with chemicals to protect them against pests and fungi.

with a high yield of leaves.

Tea planters have other things to worry about. Their crops can be attacked by various pests and diseases. One is a fungus called 'blister blight'. As its unpleasant name suggests, this creates blisters on the leaves, so ruining the crop. Other types of fungus live in the soil and attack the tea plant's roots. Small mites and beetles, which bore holes in the stems of tea plants to lay their eggs, are yet another harmful menace.

Plants can be protected against pests and fungi by spraying with certain chemicals. But planters must be careful about this. Too much spraying will spoil the quality of the leaves and the flavour of the tea we drink.

5. Pruning the bushes

As we have read on page 7, tea plants, when left to themselves, grow into trees. These are attractive to look at; but their leaves, generally, are too old and tough for making tea, as well as being too difficult to pick. That is why plants for actual tea production are cultivated as small bushes, about 1 metre (nearly 4 feet) high.

They are kept at this height by regular pruning. The main object is to trim the plant so that its branches spread out to form a fairly broad, flat top to the bush. This is called the 'plucking

These tea bushes have recently been pruned. They are growing on a plantation in Kenya.

table'. As the name suggests, its main purpose is to produce a good spread of leaves at just the right height to be picked. Regular pruning also encourages the growth of tender new shoots and leaves.

In fact, even with regular pruning, the bush,

with its plucking table, will gradually grow taller, so that after a few years it will need to be 'collar pruned' – cut right back to about 60 cm (2 feet) above the ground.

A healthy tea bush grows a 'flush', or full complement of new leaves, about once every forty days during the main growing season. The leaves are serrated (slightly saw-toothed), round the edges, and shaped quite like the head of a spear. They range from 4 to 25 cm (1½ inches to 10 inches) in length. The older leaves are also quite thick, smooth and leathery.

Regular pruning produces a good spread of leaves at just the right height for easy picking. The broad, flat top to each bush is called the 'plucking table'.

6. Growing new bushes

So it is bushes that produce the leaves that make tea we drink. A few specimens, though, are allowed to grow into flowering trees, since the bushes do not normally flower, and without these there would be no new supply of seeds.

The seeds of *camellia sinensis* are first planted in nursery greenhouses, where both temperature and humidity are closely controlled, in order to make them germinate quickly and start growing into vigorous young plants. When they are about three years old, the plants are removed from the greenhouse and replanted in the open air, to form a new tea plantation.

Rows of young tea bushes growing on a plantation in Kenya.

Tea pickers are paid according to the weight of leaves they have picked during the day.

Tea planters can obtain new bushes by other means. They may take cuttings from existing plants and place these in suitable soil. All being well, the cuttings will produce roots of their own and carry on growing.

A special variation of this method is called 'branch layering'. The planter simply bends down a branch from a fully grown bush, until it can be embedded in the earth. When this has taken root, it is severed from the parent bush and replanted.

Though fresh supplies of seed are vital, planters often prefer to take cuttings, or practise branch layering, when they can, because such cuttings and shoots are like an extension of existing plants. Growing from seed is more like starting all over again.

17

7. Leaf classification

At certain times of the year, tea bushes sprout buds and grow new leaves. The leaves are picked at these times. This is a plantation in China.

Tea plants are evergreens – they do not shed their leaves in winter, as do most trees and bushes in colder climates. But, like cocoa and many other tropical and sub-tropical trees and plants, they do go through phases of what is called 'rhythmic periodicity'. This means there are some times of the year when they sprout buds and grow new leaves much faster than at others. It is during the periods of rapid growth that the leaves are gathered, to be made into tea.

18

The leaves themselves are classified by name, according to their age and size on the bush. The youngest, smallest and tenderest are called 'pekoe'. This word comes from the Chinese *Pei Hao*, meaning 'white hair', which describes the velvety-white down covering them. Others are named 'first souchong' and 'second souchong'. This word 'souchong' is likewise derived from the Chinese – *Hsiao Chung*, meaning 'small sort'.

Such classification is important to the industry, as the size and condition of the leaves has much to do with the manufacture of the tea. The names 'pekoe' and 'souchong' are also commonly used as a part of brand names, though in the commercial sense they are used more loosely, and do not necessarily describe the type of leaves as originally plucked from the bush.

These pickers in Sri Lanka prepare to take their heavily laden baskets of tea leaves down to the weighing point.

8. Picking the leaves

Most tea bushes start going into commercial production when they are five years old. With care and attention, they will go on producing leaves for the next thirty or forty years. During their periods of rapid growth, they may produce enough new ones to be harvested once a week. And during a whole growing season, each bush should produce enough young leaves to make about 2 kg (nearly 5 lb) of finished tea.

Today there are mechanical shears for cutting the leaves from each bush. They do the job quickly, and save the planter from having to employ a large number of people to pluck the leaves by hand. Many planters, though, never use them. They can easily remove too many leaves at a time, and may also damage them. For the production of quality teas, there is still no alternative to the traditional method of picking

Tea-harvesting machines at work in the Republic of Georgia in the USSR.

the leaves by hand.

The pickers move slowly down the rows of bushes, baskets strapped to their backs. For production of the very best quality teas, they select only the bud and the two youngest leaves from each stem or twig. This is called 'fine plucking'. In the case of what is called 'medium plucking' and 'coarse plucking', they will pick the third and then the fourth leaf of each stem also.

The fact that so many people have to be employed, selecting and gathering only the best few leaves from each bush, explains why high-quality teas are expensive to buy.

To produce the best-quality teas, only the bud and the two youngest leaves (as in the picture) are picked. This is called 'fine plucking'.

9. Crushing, tearing and curling

Only about a quarter of each freshly picked leaf is solid matter, composed of fibre, cellulose and protein. The rest is sap, that is, water containing solutions of tannin, caffeine, gum and sugar.

As soon as they are brought in from the plantations, the leaves are 'withered' – spread out thinly on canvas or nylon-mesh sheets and left to dry for about twenty-four hours. This reduces their water content and concentrates the strength of their sap, or juices.

Next, the partially dried leaves are fed through machines which crush, roll and break them up. One type of machine now used in many tea-processing plants or factories is a kind of mincer called a Rotorvane. It is a large revolving drum with sharp rotating knife edges, or vanes, inside it. The leaves are packed into the drum, to be spun round and chopped into small pieces.

Below left   *A Rotorvane machine in action.*
Below right   *A Crushing, Tearing and Curling machine.*

After being picked, the leaves are brought to a factory, like this one in Sri Lanka.

Another machine is called a CTC — short for Crushing, Tearing and Curling. This is a bit like a large mangle. It has two rollers with rough surfaces, each moving at different speeds, so that the surfaces scrape against each other, twisting and crushing the leaves as they are fed through.

Described thus, it sounds as though the leaves get pretty rough treatment. In reality, the machines are designed to cut, roll and squeeze them just enough to release their juices, without undue crushing or bruising.

So they are made ready for the most important part of the whole tea-making process — the fermentation.

10. Fermentation into black tea

The crushed and fragmented leaves are laid out on large metal trays in special air-conditioned rooms, where a fairly high degree of humidity, or dampness, is maintained. This moist atmosphere encourages the leaves' sap, or juices, to ferment.

Fermentation is one of the most widespread of all chemical actions. It is caused by the presence of certain chemical 'agents', called enzymes, and it 'breaks down', or changes, the chemical composition of substances. One of the best-known kinds of fermentation converts sugar into alcohol, so producing wine and beer.

In the case of the fragmented tea leaves, the sap changes their chemical composition by absorbing oxygen from the surrounding moist air. In the process, they become sticky, turn dark brown, and take on the taste and aroma that we recognize as tea.

This fermentation goes on for about three hours. Then the trays are quickly placed in big drying chambers, in which currents of hot air are blown across the fermenting leaf fragments. The hot air stops the whole process, turns the

This machine is used to dry the leaves after they have fermented.

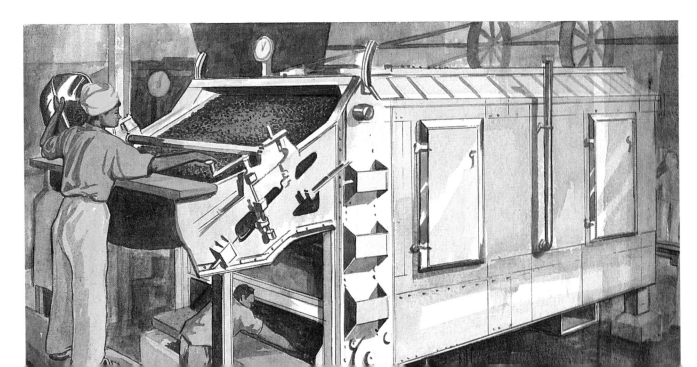

leaves crisp and dry, and seals in the flavour and colour of the fermented juices.

So we have what is termed 'black' tea – the most familiar form of the beverage. When we brew a pot of it, or soak a tea bag in boiling water, we are releasing again the colour and flavour of those fermented and dried juices.

Left   *This worker in a tea factory is preparing tea leaves for fermentation.*

Below   *A careful eye is kept on the rows of fermenting tea leaves.*

11. Grading and packing

Black tea soon loses its freshness if left exposed to the air. It cannot even be stored for too long without some loss of strength and flavour. So, the harvesting, processing, packing and marketing of tea is all done as speedily as possible.

In the first place, it is quickly graded according to size. Mechanical sieves separate the largest from the smallest fragments of leaf, and deposit them in different containers. The largest and usually the best fragments are known as 'broken leaf'. Smaller pieces are called 'fannings'. Much of the remaining dust is nowadays used to fill tea bags.

The freshly produced tea is then sold and bought at auctions held regularly, often weekly, round the year. Anyone can bid at such auctions. In practice, agents representing the big firms in the main tea-drinking countries buy up most of the fresh supplies.

After it has been sold, the tea is exported without delay. It is still packed, as it has been for a long time past, in large, square, but light-weight wooden boxes, called tea 'chests'. Today, these are lined with aluminium foil. When the lids of the chests are nailed down, the foil makes them virtually airtight, so preserving as much as possible of the tea's freshness and flavour.

The full tea chests form a light cargo, but a bulky one. So nearly all tea is still transported around the world, as it always has been, by ship.

A tea auction in progress.

Above *This machine sorts tea leaves.*   **Below** *This machine grades tea.*

12. Tea tasting

Samples of various types of tea being tasted. A taster may have to report on several hundred samples before an auction.

Some of the most important people in the tea industry are the tasters, many of whom are employed by the big tea firms. Before each auction they have a very busy time, reporting on the quality and characteristics of the various consignments of tea coming up for sale.

The taster samples a brew of each type of tea. These are prepared very carefully to standard specifications. About three grammes of each sample tea are measured out, over which about 150 millilitres of boiling water are poured. The brew is then covered and left standing for five or six minutes.

These samples are lined up in rows, each in its bowl, from which the tasters take experimental sips with a spoon. Like wine tasters, they never swallow the samples, as this would quickly dull their palate and prevent them from judging and reporting fairly on further samples. They roll each sip around their mouth, then spit it out.

Before a big auction, a taster, with his assistants, may have to report on several hundred sample brews. He will comment not only on the flavour, aroma and colour of the brew itself, but will examine the dry leaves from which it was made. He will also report on their texture and fragrance.

Tea tasters at work in a tea warehouse in New York city in 1876. Compare this with modern-day tasters on the opposite page.

13. Blending

Samples of different grades of tea in a tea factory on Java, in Indonesia.

The greatest judgment and experience of all is required of tasters who specialize in blending.

There are hundreds of varieties of tea produced around the world, and most commercial brands are a mixture or blend of them. It is the blender's job to sample new deliveries – which can vary in quality and character even when they come from the same plantation – and prescribe a blend that will retain as closely as possible the qualities of taste, aroma and appearance of an established brand.

Most blends are composed of a bulk of standard quality tea, made up with smaller amounts of high-quality tea, to give the brand its own special character, and the customer the best value for money.

Some brands also have small quantities of herbs or aromatic oils added, to give them their distinctive fragrance and flavour. This is something else the blender attends to.

He may even consider whether a particular area has hard or soft water, and how this will affect the tea, when making up a brand.

Once the blender has done his job, quantities of the various teas are measured out according to his specifications and thoroughly mixed in a large revolving drum. Then the prepared brand of tea is given a final sifting, to remove any impurities, such as pieces of stalk, mechanically measured out and packaged on long conveyor belts – ready for the last stage of its long journey from plantation to our kitchen cupboard.

Tea is still transported around the world in tea chests aboard ships.

14. Green tea

So far we have been talking about the production of black tea, which is what most of us drink today. But in China, the original home of tea, the so-called 'green' variety is still the favourite.

To make green tea, the freshly picked leaves are lightly roasted in a hot pan; or, in the case of larger quantities, they may be scalded by steam in a perforated drum. Such treatment destroys the enzyme needed for fermentation to take place. It also turns the leaves a crisp, greenish-yellow, hence the name given to the tea. The resultant brew, of a similar colour, has a somewhat bitter flavour. Today, some green teas are becoming popular outside China, bearing such interesting trade names as 'gunpowder' and 'pea leaf'.

There is also 'oolong' tea, which is semi-fermented, and is therefore a cross between black and green tea. Most oolong tea comes from Taiwan (formerly called Formosa). A special form of it is 'pouchong' tea, in which the leaves are mixed with fragrant blossoms of gardenia or jasmine.

In parts of Asia and the Far East, tea has also been treated as a food as well as a drink. People in China, Tibet and Mongolia sometimes compress tea leaves into cakes or bricks, cutting off chunks to boil up and eat with butter or cheese. A speciality of Burma is to steam the leaves, then deposit them in bamboo-lined pits for several months, after which they are eaten as a kind of pickle.

Green tea has a more bitter flavour than the more familiar 'brown' teas.

Green tea being dried in China.

15. From China to Europe

As we have just read, the long story of tea began in China. According to legend, its fragrant properties were first discovered by a Chinese emperor, or philosopher, about four thousand years ago. He was said to be sitting under a tree of *camellia sinensis*, when some of its leaves accidentally fell into a pot of boiling water.

Whatever the truth of this may be, the first recorded facts about tea come from China, dating from 400 BC. Tea drinking certainly has played a big part in the life of both China, and then of Japan, for well over a thousand years. Indeed, tea as a commodity was so highly valued in those parts that it was sometimes used

Tea was first drunk in Britain in coffee houses, like this seventeenth-century London one.

A Japanese tea market in the nineteenth century.

for barter, like salt.

It was not until the sixteenth century AD that news of tea reached people in Europe. An Italian geographer and Venetian government official, Giovanni Battista Ramuso, who compiled an edition of Marco Polo's travels to China, first mentioned it in 1559. In 1598 came the first printed reference to tea in the English language.

Dutch sailors were probably the first to bring samples of tea to Europe, about the year 1610; and in 1657 tea was first publicly sold in London, where coffee was already a popular beverage. Three years later, Samuel Pepys, from whom we know so much about daily life in seventeenth-century London, made a note of tea drinking in his famous diary.

35

16. The Boston Tea Party

Americans, disguised as Indians, throwing a cargo of tea into Boston harbour during the famous 'tea party' on 16 December 1773.

For the next hundred years or so, tea drinking in Europe was a luxury, enjoyed only by the rich, or by such famous people of the age as Dr Samuel Johnson. He was reported sometimes to drink twenty cups at a time!

Nearly all tea was still imported from China, and was often sold with expensive little oriental tea pots. Some of it was brewed in large quantities and stored in barrels, to be drawn off and heated up again, as required. For those who wanted to keep their own tea leaves, there were other expensively decorated jars, or bins, called 'caddies'.

Only towards the end of the eighteenth century did the price of tea begin to come down, so that more people could afford to drink it. It was at this time that tea played a part in one of the most dramatic episodes in world history. A tax on tea was one of many things that angered British people in the American colonies, and led to worsening relations between them and the government in London.

In 1773, as an act of protest against the way the British government was treating them, a group of American colonists, disguised as Red Indians, boarded ships at anchor in Boston harbour and tipped their cargoes of tea into the water. This event, known as the 'Boston Tea Party', was an historical landmark, leading up to the American War of Independence (or War of the Revolution) and to the Declaration of Independence in 1776.

A cartoon showing Bostonians forcing tea down the throat of a tarred-and-feathered British tax collector.

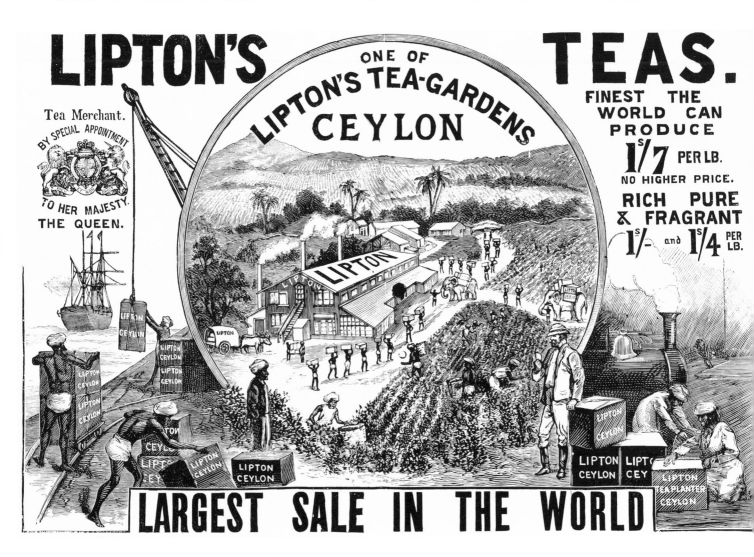

A nineteenth-century advertisement for Lipton's teas. Ceylon is the old name for the island of Sri Lanka.

The big growth in the tea trade during the nineteenth century created one of the most romantic and exciting chapters in the story of the sea and ships.

American shipbuilders started constructing vessels specially to transport tea from China to their own country and to Europe. They had long, streamlined hulls and carried a great expanse of sail on their three tall masts. They were known as 'clippers', because they were designed to 'clip', or get the very last ounce of speed out of the wind, and were among the most beautiful sailing ships ever built.

British shipyards were soon building their own clippers, and a great rivalry grew up among them, to carry cargoes of tea in the fastest possible time. The first consignment of a new tea

The tea clipper 'Anglesey' under full sail.

crop to reach London or Boston could make a fortune for the ship owners.

The captains of the tea clippers were some of the most skilled and daring sailors of their age. They were also very tough and ruthless men, who often drove their crews to the point of exhaustion.

In 1866 there was a famous race between three of them, each making the journey halfway round the world from the Chinese port of Foochow to London in 98 days. The fastest lap was 328 nautical miles in 24 hours.

The growing power and size of steamships ended the glamorous days of the clippers.

18. Expansion of the industry

While the clippers raced to and from China, planters were starting to grow tea elsewhere. Some of the first were Dutch settlers on the island of Java and other parts of what were then the Dutch East Indies (now called Indonesia).

British planters turned to India, already a big part of their empire, and by 1840 were cultivating varieties of tea bushes that grew faster and produced more leaves than the older Chinese varieties. Tea growing spread to the neighbouring island of Sri Lanka (then called Ceylon) after a blight had destroyed the coffee crops. By 1890, Ceylon was another leading tea-producing country.

By the beginning of this century, more planters were growing tea in Kenya, Tanzania and other British colonies in Africa. Parts of South America, too, have become important tea-producing regions.

For a long time now, the British have been among the world's leading tea drinkers, consuming nearly one-third of the entire world supply. Their favourite is Indian tea, of the Assam or Darjeeling varieties, which they usually drink with milk and sugar.

But tea drinking has played an interesting part in the lives of other nations, besides China and Japan. The samovar, an elaborate kind of tea kettle, is a traditional symbol of tea drinking in Russia, where tea is taken with sugar, lemon or jam.

Iced tea is an American idea; so, too, are tea bags. These were first introduced by Thomas Sullivan, an American wholesaler, who sent out trade samples in little silk bags instead of the more usual tins.

A nineteenth-century Russian tea shop with its traditional samovar (copper tea urn).

Above *Brooke Bond's famous chimpanzees are used to advertise their brands of teas.*

Below *Tea-time for an Englishman in India at the turn of the century.*

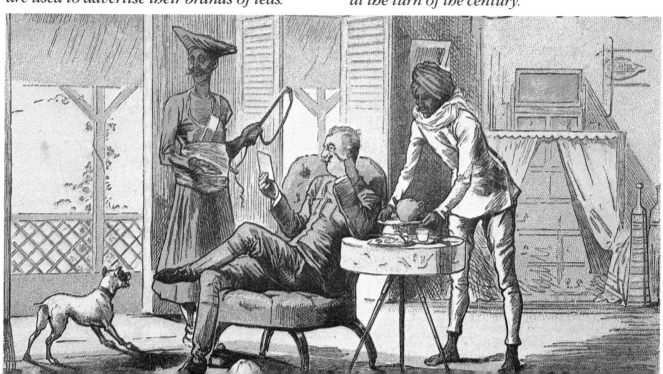

19. Tea drinking as an art

Today we take our tea for granted. But, as we have read, it was once a costly and highly-prized commodity. Moreover, in China and Japan it has long been praised for what are claimed to be its health-giving properties.

This reverence inspired the famous tea-drinking ceremony, known as the *Cha-no-yu*, or 'Way of Tea', which is still a fascinating part of Japanese life. It is closely connected with the Buddhist religion, which spread from China to Japan about 800 years ago. Japanese Zen Buddhist monks took tea as a stimulant, to prevent drowsiness during long hours of meditation; and it was they who turned the drinking of it into a form of ritual.

The traditional setting is a tea house, or *sukiya*. This is a fairly small room, with paper-covered windows to create a soft, warm light,

A picture of the Mad Hatter's tea party from Lewis Carroll's 'Alice in Wonderland'.

Two Japanese students learning the art of the tea ceremony.

and such simple decoration as flower arrangements and scrolls of beautiful brush-stroke writing.

The ritual of brewing and drinking the tea is intended to express the four Buddhist principles of harmony, respect, purity and tranquillity, leading to peace of mind and spirit.

Those taking part bow low to each other, speak quietly, praising the flowers and scrolls in the tea house, and then the delicate fragrance and flavour of the tea, which is dispensed in little porcelain cups or bowls.

No other food or drink has been treated with such ceremony and respect as tea!

Facts and figures

How tea got its name

Both the 'correct' name, tea, and the British 'slang' word, Cha, come from two versions of the original Chinese word for tea. The Chinese version *T'e* (pronounced Tay) was adopted by the traders who first introduced tea to Britain. This is how we get the word 'tea'.

The other Chinese version, *C'ha*, was used by people in India when tea was introduced there. The word became Cha, and the many British troops of the Indian Army stationed in India during the nineteenth and early twentieth centuries got used to calling for their 'cup of Cha'. When these soldiers returned home, they continued to call their tea by this name.

Important dates

4th century BC	Earliest known mention of tea, in China.
8th century AD	By this time, tea drinking was widespread in China, both as a beverage and for its medicinal properties.
AD 805	Tea seeds introduced into Japan by Buddhist priests who had been in China.
1559	First mention of tea in European writings.
1610	First samples of tea reached Europe.
1657	At about this time, tea reached Britain and America. It sold in Britain for £10 per pound.
1660	Charles II of Britain put a tax on tea.
1773	King George III imposed a tax on all tea imported into British colonies in America. This sparked off the Boston Tea Party.
1788	Tea introduced into India.
1842	The first tea seeds planted in Ceylon (Sri Lanka).
1843	The American tea clipper *Rainbow* did a return journey from New York to Canton, in China, in under 200 days.
1850	The first British tea clipper, *Stornaway*, was launched.
1871	Last clipper race.
1880	Around this time, tea shops began to be opened in towns and cities in Britain.
1925	Tea planted in Kenya, followed shortly afterwards by Uganda, Tanzania and Zimbabwe.

Where does Britain's tea come from?

Britain imports more tea than any other country in the world – over 25 per cent of the entire world's exports of tea. The diagram on the right shows the proportion of tea imported into Britain from the producing countries.

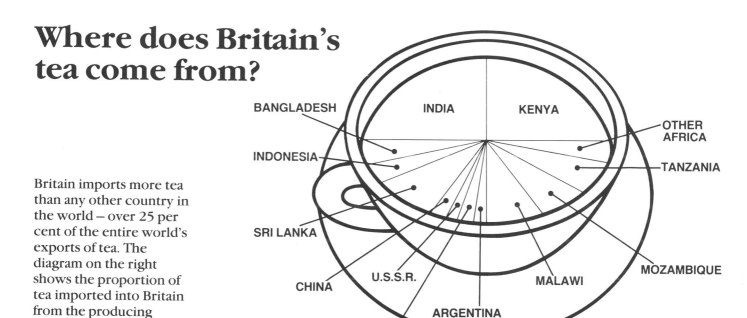

Tea consumption around the world

Major tea-consuming countries
(consumption in thousands of metric tonnes)

1.	India	301
2.	Britain	185
3.	USSR	141
4.	Japan	113
5.	USA	81
6.	Pakistan	56
7.	Indonesia	40
8.	Iran	28
9.	Egypt	27
10.	Australia	24

Average tea consumption per person
(consumption in kg per annum)

1.	Irish Republic	3.5
2.	Britain	3.3
3.	New Zealand	2.4
4.	Turkey	2.0
5.	Hong Kong	1.8
6.	Australia	1.7
7.	Sri Lanka	1.5
8.	Tunisia	1.2
9.	Jordan	1.0
10.	Chile	1.0

Glossary

Assam An Indian variety of tea, originally grown in the region of Assam, now to the north of the state of Bangladesh.

Barter To exchange goods without any money payment.

Beverage Refreshing or stimulating drink, either alcoholic, or such drinks as tea and coffee.

Black tea Varieties of tea made by fermenting the leaves until they turn a brownish-black colour. The most popular form of tea today.

Blend A carefully calculated mixture of different varieties of tea. Most trade brands of tea are blends.

Brew Method of fermenting barley malt to make beer; or a general term to describe the soaking or infusing of tea leaves in boiling water.

Cellulose Substance forming the basic structure of plant life.

Clipper Very fast type of merchant sailing ship, used in the nineteenth century mainly to transport tea from China to Europe and North America.

Compost Type of manure, mostly made from decaying vegetable matter.

Darjeeling An Indian variety of tea, originally grown in the vicinity of Darjeeling, in the foothills of the Himalayas.

Enzyme That part of a chemical substance that acts as an 'agent', allowing fermentation to take place.

Fermentation Type of chemical action which changes the composition of a substance.

Germinate To begin to grow or to sprout, especially when talking about a seed.

Green tea Original Chinese and Japanese type of tea, made by roasting the leaves instead of allowing them to ferment.

Gum A sticky substance.

Oolong Type of tea, made by allowing the leaves partly to ferment and then stopping the process. The resulting tea is a cross between black and green tea.

Pekoe Name for the smallest leaves on a tea bush. From the Chinese *Pei Hao* – 'white hair' – describing the soft down still on them.

Perforated A material pierced with holes.

Porcelain Very fine, delicate type of earthenware material, traditionally made in China.

Pruning Trimming or cutting off portions of a plant to make it grow a certain way.

Samovar Type of tea kettle or urn, traditionally used in Russia to make tea.

Souchong Name for some of the leaves on a tea bush. From the Chinese *Hsiao Chung* – 'small sort'.

Sources for further information

For more facts and figures about tea, in Britain you can contact:

The Tea Council Ltd
Sir John Lyon House
5 High Timber Street
London EC4V 3NJ

If you live in North America, you can contact:

The Tea Association of the USA
230 Park Avenue
New York City

Books to read

BRAMAH, E. *Tea and Coffee* (Hutchinson, 1972)
JOEL, D. & SCHAPIRA K. *The Book of Coffee and Tea* (St Martin's Press, New York, 1975)
LANGLEY, A. *A Cup of Tea* (Wayland, 1982)
PITT, V. *A First Look at Tea* (Franklin Watts, 1982)
SMITH, M. *Tea* (Ladybird Leaders, 1981)

Picture acknowledgements

The author and the publishers would like to thank the following for loaning illustrations for this book: Brooke Bond Oxo Ltd 41 (top); Michael MacIntyre (32), Lesley Nelson (13, 18), Mick Rook (11, 17) all from Camerapix Hutchison Library; Peter Davey (14), L. R. Dawson (6), Michael Freeman (15), C. B. & D. W. Frith (8 right, 30), Jennifer Fry (8 left), M. Timothy O'Keefe (33) all from Bruce Coleman Ltd; Mary Evans Picture Library 42; Fotomas Index 34; Peter Newark's WESTERN AMERICANA 29, 35, 36, 37, 38, 40, 41 (bottom); the Tea Council 21, 22 (both), 25 (both), 26, 27 (both), 28, 31, 45; Malcolm Walker 9; Wayland Picture Library 10, 20, 24, 39, 43; Stephen White-Thompson *cover*; ZEFA 19, 23.

Index